SPOTLIGHT SOLOS

VOLUME ONE

Showcase Solos for All Ages

Music by

Jennifer Eklund

PianoPronto.com

Spotlight Solos: Volume One

Jennifer Eklund

Copyright ©2014 by Piano Pronto Publishing, Inc.
Second edition copyright ©2021 by Piano Pronto Publishing, Inc.

ISBN 978-0-9899084-7-4

Printed in the United States of America.

Piano Pronto Publishing, Inc.
PianoPronto.com

SPOTLIGHT SOLOS

VOLUME ONE

Showcase Solos for All Ages

Music by

Jennifer Eklund

PianoPronto.com

1

SOMEDAY

Jennifer Eklund

Moderately slow

poco rit.

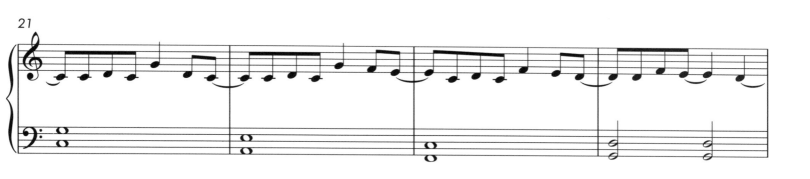

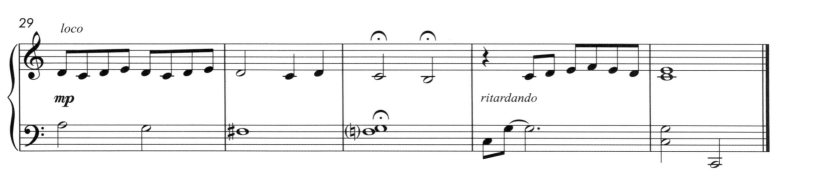

SPANISH DANCE

Jennifer Eklund

END GAME

Jennifer Eklund

Quickly

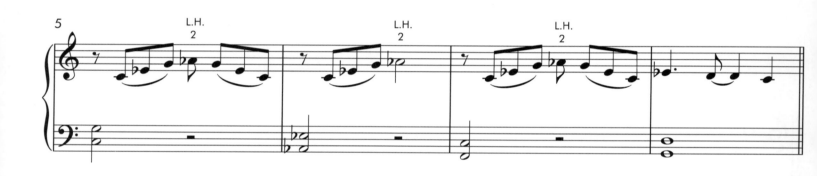

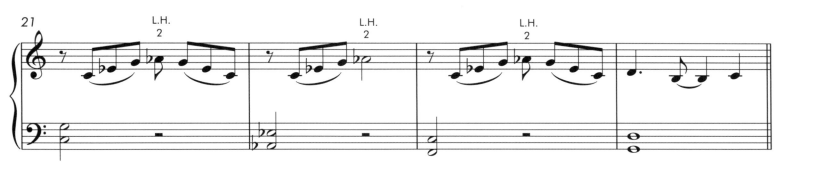

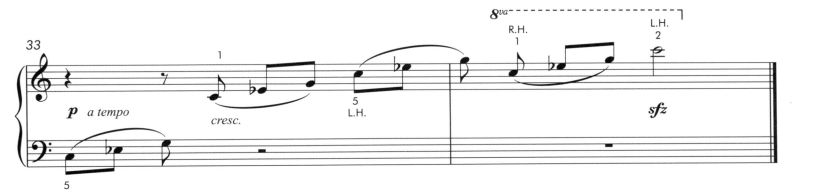

THE RETURN

Jennifer Eklund

Moderately

p

with pedal

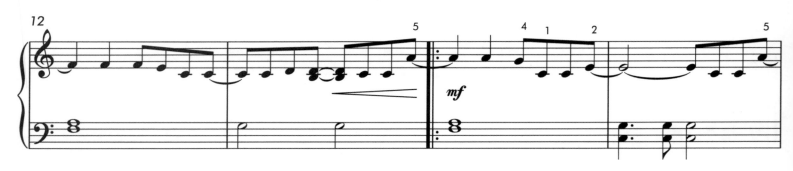

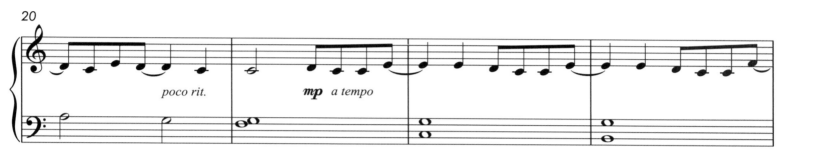

No Limits

Jennifer Eklund

Fast

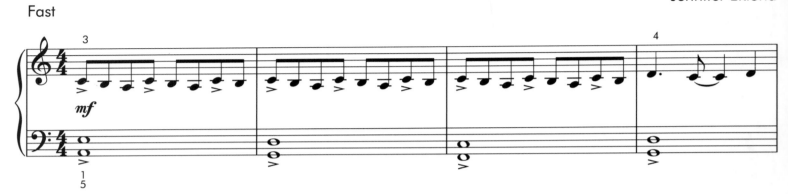

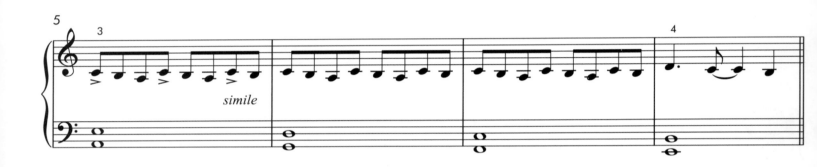

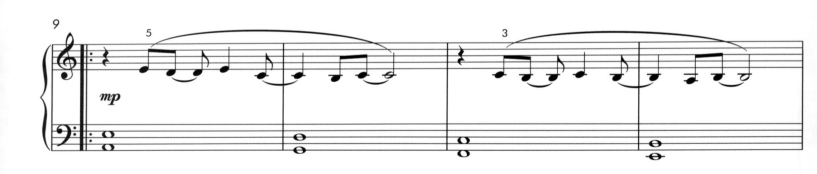

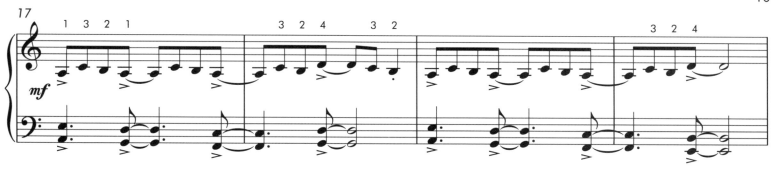

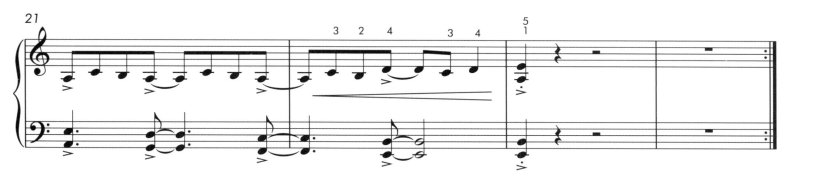

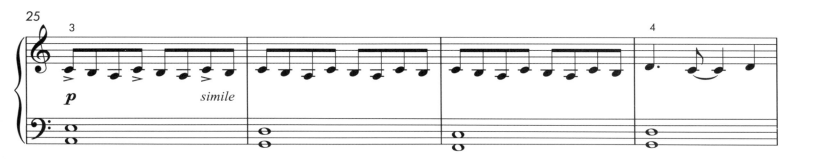

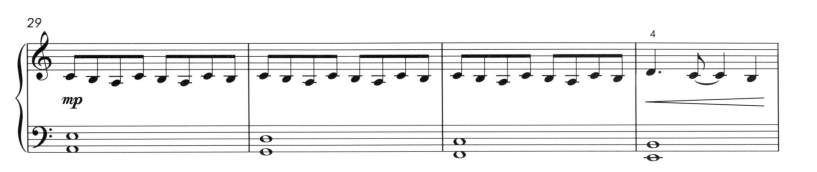

Bluesy Tuesday

Jennifer Eklund

Heavy swing

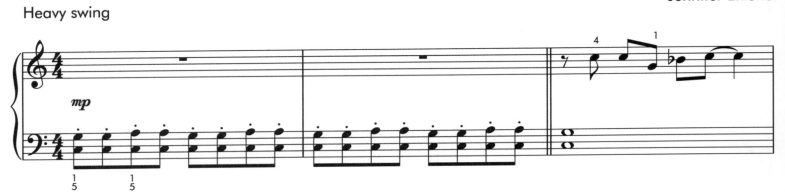

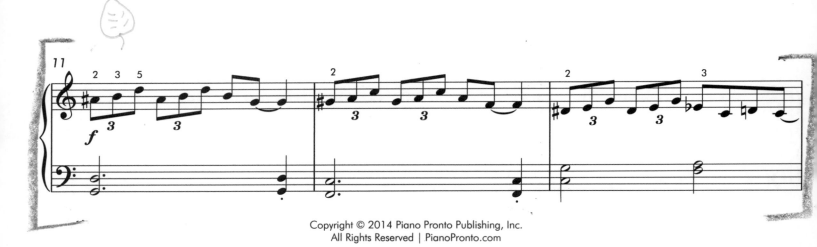

Super Spy Guy

Jennifer Eklund

Oh Snap!

Jennifer Eklund

Moderate swing

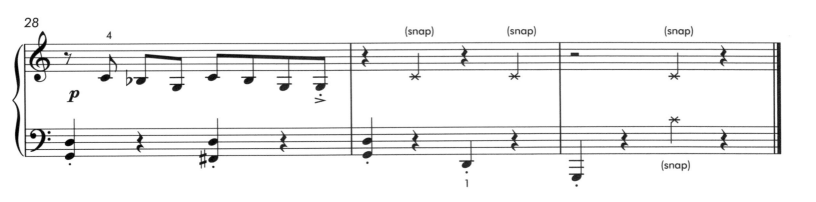

SKIPPING TOWN

Jennifer Eklund

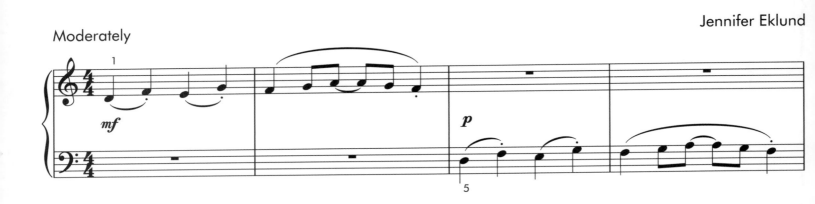

THE CHASE

Jennifer Eklund

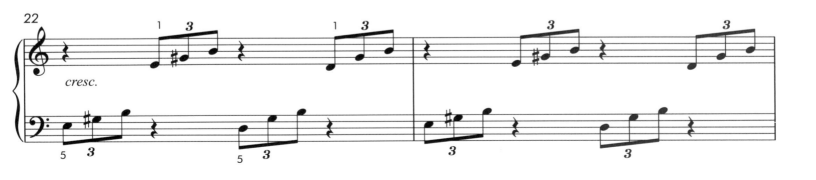

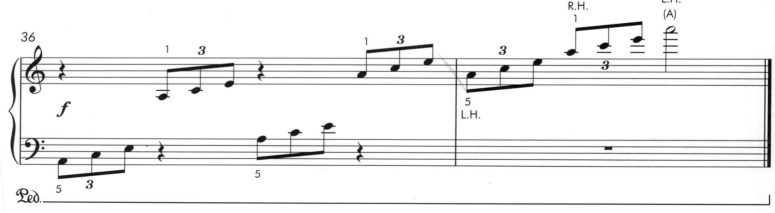